What's the Difference Between a Dolphin and a Porpoise?

by Trisha Speed Shaskan

illustrated by Bandelin-Dacey

PICTURE WINDOW BOOKS
a capstone imprint

Thanks to our advisers for their expertise, research, and advice:

Christine DeAngelo
Associate Curator of Mammals
Monterey Bay Aquarium, Monterey, California

Terry Flaherty, PhD, Professor of English
Minnesota State University, Mankato

Editor: Shelly Lyons
Designer: Matt Bruning
Art Director: Nathan Gassman
Page Production: Jane Klenk
The illustrations in this book were created with watercolor.

Photo credit: Shutterstock/siloto (handmade paper), 1 (background)
and throughout in sidebars and titlebars

Picture Window Books
151 Good Counsel Drive
P.O. Box 669
Mankato, MN 56002-0669
877-845-8392
www.capstonepub.com

Printed in the United States of America in North Mankato, Minnesota.
032010
005740CGF10

 All books published by Picture Window Books are manufactured with paper containing at least 10 percent post-consumer waste.

Library of Congress Cataloging-in-Publication Data
Shaskan, Trisha Speed, 1973–
What's the difference between a dolphin and a porpoise? / by Trisha Speed Shaskan ; illustrated by Bandelin-Dacey.
    p. cm. — (What's the difference?)
 Includes index.
 ISBN 978-1-4048-5545-8 (library binding)
 1. Dolphins—Juvenile literature. 2. Porpoises—Juvenile literature.
I. Bandelin, Debra, ill. II. Dacey, Bob, ill. III. Title.
QL737.C432S485 2011
 599.53—dc22   2010000901

A dolphin and a porpoise slip beneath the water's surface. Both of these mammals are classified under the order cetacea. Cetaceans have long, slim, hairless bodies. They have a fluke, a blowhole, and no hind limbs. But dolphins and porpoises have some differences. Can you spot them?

A dolphin will swim near shore or in deeper water. It has a long, sleek body. From above, the dolphin's dark gray back blends in with the water's surface. From below, its white belly shows brightly like the sun on the water.

A porpoise stays near the shore. It is smaller and chubbier than a dolphin. Its dark brown back is hard to see in the water.

dolphin

Many dolphins and porpoises live in saltwater. But some of them, such as the finless porpoise, can also live in freshwater rivers.

porpoise

A dolphin has a beaklike snout called a rostrum. At the top of its head is a blowhole. The dolphin breathes in a gas called oxygen through the hole. It closes the blowhole when it goes underwater.

rostrum

blowhole

A porpoise's head is rounded and does not have a rostrum. Like a dolphin, a porpoise breathes through a blowhole.

blowhole

Dolphins and porpoises are warm-blooded. That means their body temperature remains about the same.

Dolphins and porpoises have pectoral flippers, a dorsal fin, and a tail fluke to help them to move through the water. The flippers help them to steer and stop. The dorsal fins keep the animals steady in the water. The animals move their tail flukes up and down to push themselves through the water.

dorsal fins

tail flukes

The dolphin's dorsal fin is curved toward its tail. A porpoise's dorsal fin points upward and is shaped like a triangle.

pectoral flippers

Some dolphins and porpoises have no dorsal fins.

Dolphins and porpoises are vertebrates. They have a backbone. A dolphin's backbone can bend. The animal can move its head from side to side.

A porpoise's backbone can't bend as well. Its first six vertebrae are small and stuck together. It's difficult for the animal to move its neck.

A young dolphin or porpoise is called a calf. It swims so close to its mother that it looks like a part of her. Both the mother and the calf belong to a group of dolphins or porpoises called a pod.

Members of the pod help one another if one of them is hurt or in trouble. If a dolphin gets lost from its group, it whistles to the others. The group members recognize the animal's sound and whistle back. Then the lost animal can find its friends.

Each dolphin makes a different whistling sound. This special sound is called a signature whistle.

Instead of trying to see their way through water, dolphins and porpoises use sound. They make loud clicks that bounce off objects, or echo. This process is called echolocation.

A hungry dolphin or porpoise will use clicks to search for food. The loud clicks will bounce off fish and other animals. The dolphin or porpoise can follow the echo to find its prey.

echo

clicks from porpoise

A dolphin has cone-shaped teeth. The animal uses its teeth to grab a fish. Then it swallows the fish whole.

Dolphins and porpoises are meat-eaters, or carnivores. They eat mostly fish and squid.

A hungry porpoise catches a squid with its spade-shaped teeth. A porpoise swallows the squid whole.

Dolphins like to play. They might chase and splash each other. Like acrobats, they jump through the air.

Dolphins have been seen jumping as high as 16 feet (4.9 meters) into the air!

Porpoises hide near the coast. Unlike dolphins, they don't jump out of the water.

Because they are smart and like to play, dolphins are often trained to perform for people. Zoos and aquariums are popular places for people to see dolphins.

Porpoises can be trained, but they are hard to catch. For this reason, porpoises are not found in as many zoos or aquariums.

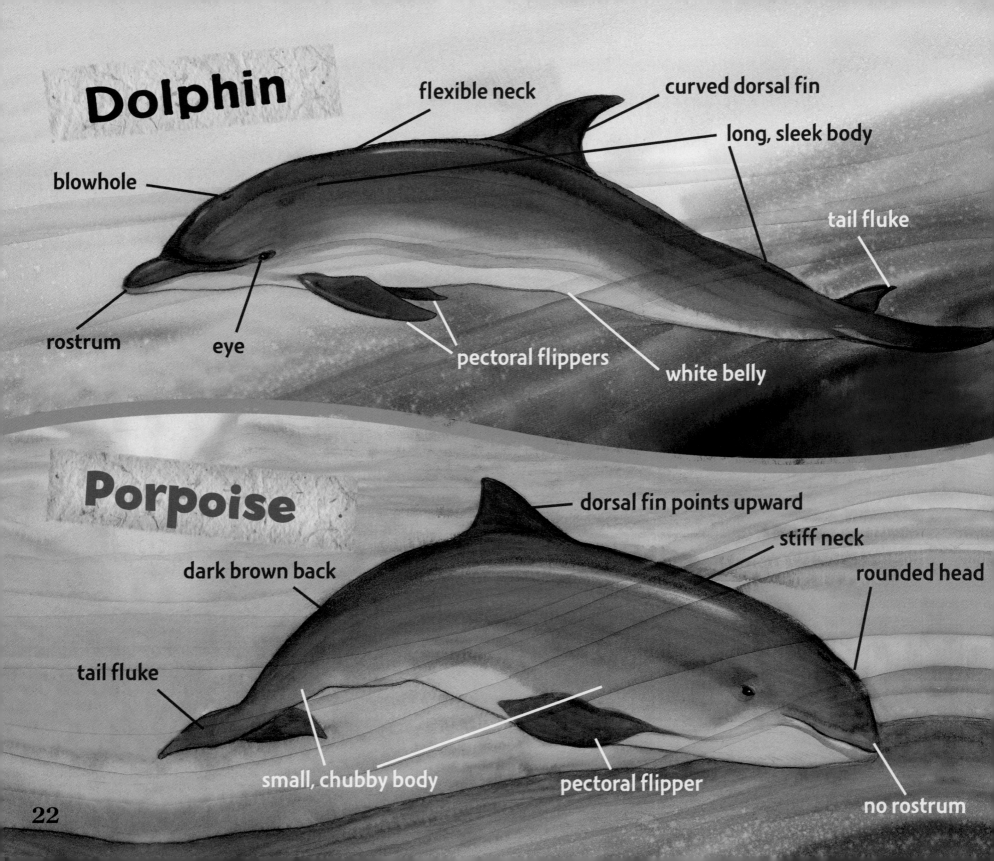

Dolphin

flexible neck

curved dorsal fin

long, sleek body

blowhole

tail fluke

rostrum

eye

pectoral flippers

white belly

Porpoise

dorsal fin points upward

stiff neck

dark brown back

rounded head

tail fluke

small, chubby body

pectoral flipper

no rostrum

Fun Facts

The largest dolphin is the Orca, or killer whale. It can be up to 28 feet (8.5 m) long and weigh as much as 6 tons (5.4 metric tons). Porpoises are much smaller. The largest porpoise, the Dall's porpoise, is about 7 feet (2.1 m) long. It weighs as much as 400 pounds (181 kilograms).

Like whales, dolphins and porpoises have blubber. Blubber is a thick layer of fat under the skin. It helps keep the animals warm.

The harbor porpoise is the most common porpoise. It has been called a puffer or a tumbler. That's because the animal makes puffing noises when it appears at the water's surface.

Dolphin pods usually have two to 15 members. Pods may join together as a larger group to help protect each other.

Glossary

blowhole—a hole on the top of a dolphin's or porpoise's head that is used for breathing

calf—a young dolphin or porpoise

cetacea—the order of mammals that includes whales, dolphins, and porpoises; animals that have a nearly hairless body, no hind limbs, a fluke, and a blowhole

dorsal fin—the fin on a dolphin's or porpoise's back

echolocation—the location of objects and direction by reflected sounds

fluke—a dolphin's or porpoise's tail fin

mammal—warm-blooded animals that have hair and drink their mother's milk when they are young

pectoral flipper—the fin on each side of a dolphin's or porpoise's body

pod—a large group of dolphins or porpoises

prey—an animal that is hunted and eaten for food

rostrum—the beaklike snout on a dolphin

vertebra—one of the small bones that make up the backbone

vertebrate—an animal that has a backbone

warm-blooded—having a body temperature that stays the same

To Learn More

More Books to Read

Edgemon, Darcie. *Seamore, the Very Forgetful Porpoise*. New York: HarperCollins Publishers, 2008.

Herriges, Ann. *Dolphins*. Oceans Alive! Minneapolis: Bellwether Media, 2007.

Rake, Jody Sullivan. *Bottlenose Dolphins Up Close*. Whales and Dolphins Up Close. Mankato, Minn.: Capstone Press, 2009

Rhodes, Mary Jo. *Dolphins, Seals, and Other Sea Mammals*. Undersea Encounters. New York: Children's Press, 2007.

Internet Sites

FactHound offers a safe, fun way to find Internet sites related to this book. All of the sites on FactHound have been researched by our staff.

Here's all you do:

Visit *www.facthound.com*

FactHound will fetch the best sites for you!

Index

Look for all the books in the What's the Difference? series:

What's the Difference Between a Butterfly and a Moth?

What's the Difference Between a Dolphin and a Porpoise?

What's the Difference Between a Frog and a Toad?

What's the Difference Between a Leopard and a Cheetah?

What's the Difference Between a Turtle and a Tortoise?

What's the Difference Between an Alligator and a Crocodile?